CREATIVE TOUCHES™

Stenciling
ETC.

THE HOME DECORATING INSTITUTE®

Copyright© 1996 Cy DeCosse Incorporated 5900 Green Oak Drive Minnetonka, Minnesota 55343
1-800-328-3895 All rights reserved Printed in U.S.A.

Library of Congress Cataloging-in-Publication Data Stenciling etc. p. cm. ISBN 0-86573-995-1 (softcover)
1. Stencil work. 2. Block printing. 3. Screen process printing. 4. Interior decoration. I. Cy DeCosse Incorporated.
TT270.S777 1996 745.7'3 — dc20 96-15849

CONTENTS

Getting Started

Stenciling

Block & Screen Printing

Stenciling
ETC.

Give your home a personal touch with unique designs on walls, furniture, and accessories. The techniques of stenciling, block printing, and screen printing offer limitless decorating possibilities, allowing you to have a designer look at a fraction of the cost. With a minimal investment in paint and materials, you can decorate your home in a style that truly reflects your individuality.

Learn basic stenciling techniques, including how to design and cut your own stencils. Use standard stenciling methods on walls, furniture, and table linens. Or, try your hand at some unique stenciling methods, including resist-stain stenciling on wood or composite metallic stenciling on decorative accessories and furniture. Even stencil a border around a sisal rug.

Design and make printing blocks from closed-cell foam for printing walls, furniture, or fabric. Develop your own silk screens for making one-of-a-kind decorator fabrics or floor cloths.

Learn these decorating techniques easily with full-color step-by-step photography. Be inspired to add your own creative touch in every room.

GETTING STARTED

Primers & Finishes

PRIMERS

Some surfaces must be coated with a primer before the paint is applied. Primers ensure good adhesion of paint and are used to seal porous surfaces so paint will spread smoothly without soaking in. It is usually not necessary to prime a nonporous surface in good condition, such as smooth, unchipped, previously painted wood or wallboard. Many types of water-based primers are available; select one that is suitable for the type of surface you are painting.

A. FLAT LATEX PRIMER is used for sealing unfinished wallboard. It makes the surface nonporous so fewer coats of paint are needed. This primer may also be used to seal previously painted wallboard before you apply new paint of a dramatically different color. The primer prevents the original color from showing through.

B. LATEX ENAMEL UNDERCOAT is used for priming most raw woods or woods that have been previously painted or stained. A wood primer closes the pores of the wood, for a smooth surface. It is not used for cedar, redwood, or plywoods that contain water-soluble dyes, because the dyes would bleed through the primer.

C. RUST-INHIBITING LATEX METAL PRIMER helps paint adhere to metal. Once a rust-inhibiting primer is applied, water-based paint may be used on metal without causing the surface to rust.

D. POLYVINYL ACRYLIC PRIMER, or PVA, is used to seal the porous surface of plaster and unglazed pottery, if a smooth paint finish is desired. To preserve the texture of plaster or unglazed pottery, apply the paint directly to the surface without using a primer.

E. STAIN-KILLING PRIMER seals stains like crayon, ink, and grease so they will not bleed through the top coat of paint. It is used to seal knotholes and is the recommended primer for cedar, redwood, and plywood with water-soluble dyes. This versatile primer is also used for glossy surfaces like glazed pottery and ceramic, making it unnecessary to sand or degloss the surface.

FINISHES

Finishes are sometimes used over paint as the final coat. They protect the painted surface with a transparent coating. The degree of protection and durability varies, from a light application of matte aerosol sealer to a glossy layer of clear finish.

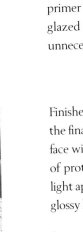

F. CLEAR FINISH, such as water-based urethanes and acrylics, may be used over painted finishes for added durability. Available in matte, satin, and gloss, these clear finishes are applied with a brush or sponge applicator. Environmentally safe clear finishes are available in pints, quarts, and gallons (0.5, 0.9, and 3.8 L) at paint supply stores and in 4-oz. and 8-oz. (119 and 237 mL) bottles or jars at craft stores.

G. AEROSOL CLEAR ACRYLIC SEALER, available in matte or gloss, may be used as the final coat over paint as a protective finish. A gloss sealer also adds sheen and depth to the painted finish for a more polished look. Apply aerosol sealer in several light coats rather than one heavy coat, to avoid dripping or puddling. To protect the environment, select an aerosol sealer that does not contain harmful propellants. Use all sealers in a well-ventilated area.

Tools & Supplies

TAPES

When painting, use tape to mask off any surrounding areas. Several brands are available, varying in the amount of tack, how well they release from the surface without damaging the base coat, and how long they can remain in place before removal. You may want to test the tape before applying it to the entire project. The edge of the tape should be sealed tightly to prevent seepage.

PAINT ROLLERS

Paint rollers are used to paint an area quickly with an even coat of paint. Roller pads, available in several nap thicknesses, are used in conjunction with roller frames. Use synthetic or lamb's wool roller pads to apply water-based paints.

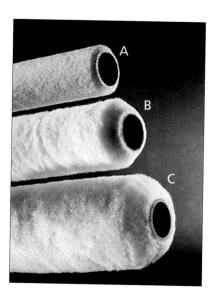

A. SHORT-NAP ROLLER PADS with 1/4" to 3/8" (6 mm to 1 cm) nap are used for applying glossy paints to smooth surfaces like wallboard, wood, and smooth plaster.

B. MEDIUM-NAP ROLLER PADS with 1/2" to 3/4" (1.3 to 2 cm) nap are used as all-purpose pads. They give flat surfaces a slight texture.

C. LONG-NAP ROLLER PADS with 1" to 1 1/4" (2.5 to 3.2 cm) nap are used to cover textured areas in fewer passes.

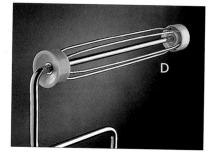

D. ROLLER FRAME is the metal arm and handle that holds the roller pad in place. A wire cage supports the pad in the middle. Select a roller frame with nylon bearings so it will roll smoothly and a threaded end on the handle so you can attach an extension pole.

E. EXTENSION POLE has a threaded end that screws into the handle of a roller frame. Use an extension pole when painting ceilings, high wall areas, and floors.

PAINTBRUSHES & APPLICATORS

Several types of paintbrushes and applicators are available, designed for various purposes. Select the correct one to achieve the best quality in the paint finish.

A. SYNTHETIC-BRISTLE paintbrushes are generally used with water-based latex and acrylic paints, while B. NATURAL-BRISTLE brushes are used with alkyd, or oil-based paints. Natural-bristle paintbrushes may be used with water-based paints to create certain decorative effects.

C. BRUSH COMBS remove dried or stubborn paint particles from paintbrushes and align the bristles so they dry properly. To use a brush comb, hold the brush in a stream of water as you pull the comb several times through the bristles from the base to the tips. Use mild soap on the brush, if necessary, and rinse well. The curved side of the tool can be used to remove paint from the roller pad.

Stencil brushes are available in a range of sizes. Use the small brushes for fine detail work in small stencil openings, and the large brushes for larger openings. Either D. SNYTHETIC or E. NATURAL-BRISTLE stencil brushes may be used with acrylic paints.

Artist's brushes are available in several types, including F. FAN, G. LINER, and H. FLAT BRUSHES. After cleaning the brushes, always reshape the head of the brush by stroking the bristles with your fingers. Store artist's brushes upright on their handles or lying flat so there is no pressure on the bristles.

I. SPONGE APPLICATORS are used for a smooth application of paint on flat surfaces.

J. PAINT EDGERS with guide wheels are used to apply paint next to moldings, ceilings, and corners. The guide wheels can be adjusted for proper alignment of the paint pad.

Preparing the Surface

To achieve a high-quality and long-lasting paint finish that adheres well to the surface, it is important to prepare the surface properly so it is clean and smooth. The preparation steps vary, depending on the type of surface you are painting. Often it is necessary to apply a primer to the surface before painting it. For more information about primers, refer to pages 8 and 9.

PREPARING SURFACES FOR PAINTING

SURFACE TO BE PAINTED	PREPARATION STEPS	PRIMER
UNFINISHED WOOD	1. Sand surface to smooth it. 2. Wipe with damp cloth to remove grit. 3. Apply primer.	Latex enamel undercoat.
PREVIOUSLY PAINTED WOOD	1. Clean surface to remove any grease and dirt. 2. Rinse with clear water; allow to dry. 3. Sand surface lightly to degloss and smooth it and to remove any loose paint chips. 4. Wipe with damp cloth to remove grit. 5. Apply primer to any areas of bare wood.	Not necessary, except to touch up areas of bare wood; then use latex enamel undercoat.
PREVIOUSLY VARNISHED WOOD	1. Clean surface to remove any grease and dirt. 2. Rinse with clear water; allow to dry. 3. Sand surface to degloss it. 4. Wipe with damp cloth to remove grit. 5. Apply primer.	Latex enamel undercoat.
UNFINSHED WALLBOARD	1. Dust with hand broom, or vacuum with soft brush attachment. 2. Apply primer.	Flat latex primer.
PREVIOUSLY PAINTED WALLBOARD	1. Clean surface to remove any grease and dirt. 2. Rinse with clear water; allow to dry. 3. Apply primer, only if making a dramatic color change.	Not necessary, except when painting over dark or strong color; then use flat latex primer.
UNPAINTED PLASTER	1. Sand any flat surfaces as necessary. 2. Dust with hand broom, or vacuum with soft brush attachment.	Polyvinyl acrylic primer.
PREVIOUSLY PAINTED PLASTER	1. Clean surface to remove any grease and dirt. 2. Rinse with clear water; allow to dry thoroughly. 3. Fill any cracks with spackling compound. 4. Sand surface to degloss it.	Not necessary, except when painting over dark or strong color; then use polyvinyl acrylic primer.
UNGLAZED POTTERY	1. Dust with brush, or vacuum with soft brush attachment. 2. Apply primer.	Polyvinyl acrylic primer or gesso.
GLAZED POTTERY, CERAMIC & GLASS	1. Clean surface to remove any grease and dirt. 2. Rinse with clear water; allow to dry thoroughly. 3. Apply primer.	Stain-killing primer.
METAL	1. Clean surface with vinegar or lacquer thinner to remove any grease and dirt. 2. Sand surface to degloss it and to remove any rust. 3. Wipe with damp cloth to remove grit. 4. Apply primer.	Rust-inhibiting latex metal primer.
FABRIC	1. Prewash fabric without fabric softener to remove any sizing, if fabric is washable. 2. Press fabric as necessary.	None.

Paints & Inks

A wide variety of paint is available from paint supply stores and craft stores. Each type has advantages that make it especially suitable for certain kinds of painting. All of the following are water-based, making cleanup easy with soap and water. Water-based paints are also safer for the environment than oil-based paints.

LATEX PAINTS

Latex paint is fast drying and durable. In addition to the wide range of premixed colors, latex paint can be custom-mixed by a paint professional. It is available in various finishes, from flat latex for a matte appearance to high-gloss latex with maximum sheen. Low-luster latex enamel paint, sometimes referred to as eggshell enamel, has some sheen and provides good coverage; semigloss has a bit more sheen. The glossier the paint, the more durable it is. Packaged in pints, quarts, and gallons (0.5, 0.9, and 3.8 L), latex paint is suitable for general use in small and large jobs.

Latex paint contains acrylic or vinyl resins or a combination of both. Latex paints of acrylic resins are the highest quality, with vinyl-acrylic blends next in quality, followed by paints consisting solely of vinyl resins. High-quality paints may cost significantly more, but they provide an even, complete coverage and wear longer.

CRAFT ACRYLIC PAINT

Craft acrylic paint contains 100 percent acrylic resins. Generally sold in 2-oz., 4-oz., and 8-oz. (59, 119, and 237 mL) bottles or jars, these premixed acrylics have a creamy brushing consistency and give excellent coverage. They should not be confused with the thicker artist's acrylics used for canvas paintings. Craft acrylic paint can be diluted with water, acrylic extender, or latex paint conditioner if a thinner consistency is desired. Craft acrylic paints are available in many colors and in metallic, fluorescent, and iridescent formulas.

SCREEN-PRINTING INK

Textile inks, available at art supply stores, are used for screen printing. They can be purchased in several opaque and transparent colors and can be mixed for greater variety.

FABRIC PAINTS

Fabric paints have been formulated specifically for painting on fabric. To prevent excessive stiffness in the painted fabric, avoid a heavy application; the texture of the fabric should show through the paint. Once the paints are heat-set with an iron, the fabric can be machine washed and dry-cleaned. Acrylic paints can also be used for fabric painting; textile medium may be added to the acrylics to make them more pliable on fabric.

STENCILING

Stenciled Designs

Use stenciled motifs to highlight an area of a room or to simulate architectural details, such as chair rails. A variety of precut stencils is available, with the prices varying widely, usually depending on the intricacy of the design. Or, custom stencils are easily made by tracing designs onto transparent Mylar® sheets. For stencils that coordinate with home furnishings, designs can be adapted from wallpaper, fabric, or artwork. Use a photocopy machine to enlarge or reduce patterns to the desired size.

Most precut stencils will have a separate plate for each color and will be numbered according to the sequence for use. A single stencil plate may be used for multiple colors if the spaces between the design areas are large enough to be covered with masking tape. When stenciling multicolored designs, apply the largest part of the design first. When stenciling borders, it is generally best to apply all the repeats of the first color before applying the second color.

Before starting a project, carefully plan the placement of the design. Stencil the design onto paper, and tape it to the surface to check the design placement. Border designs with obvious repeats, such as swags or bows, require careful planning to avoid any partial motifs. If you are stenciling a border, the placement may be influenced by the position of room details, such as windows, doors, and heat vents. It is generally best to start at the most prominent area and work out; the spacing between border repeats may be altered slightly, if necessary.

Use stiff stencil brushes of good quality and sized in proportion to the space being stenciled. Use a separate brush for each color, or clean the brush and allow it to dry before reusing it.

For painting hard surfaces, such as walls and woodwork, use craft acrylic paint or oil-based stencil paint in liquid or solid form. You may stencil over a clean, painted surface or over finished wood. If the surface is finished wood, apply a clear finish or sealer to the entire surface after it is stenciled.

For stenciling on fabric, use fabric paints or combine two parts craft acrylic paint to one part textile medium. With either choice of paint, the fabric will not be stiffened. Follow the manufacturer's directions to heat-set the paints. Select fabric that is at least 50 percent cotton, for good penetration of the paint. Avoid fabrics with polished or protective finishes. Prewash fabrics to remove any sizing.

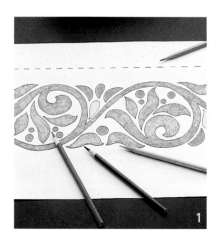

MATERIALS

GENERAL SUPPLIES

- ◆ Precut or custom stencil.
- ◆ Craft acrylic paints, or liquid or solid oil-based stencil paints.
- ◆ Stencil brushes.
- ◆ Disposable plates.
- ◆ Masking tape.
- ◆ Spray adhesive, optional.

FOR CUSTOM STENCILS

- ◆ Transparent Mylar® sheets.
- ◆ Mat knife.
- ◆ Cutting surface, such as a self-healing cutting board or cardboard.
- ◆ Colored pencils; fine-point permanent-ink marker.

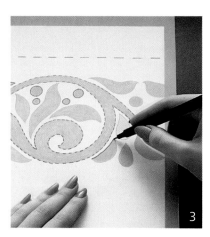

How to make a custom stencil

1. Trace design, enlarging or reducing it, if desired. Repeat the design for 13" to 18" (33 to 46 cm) length, making sure the spacing between repeats is consistent. Color the traced design as desired, using colored pencils. Mark placement lines so stencil will be correctly positioned on wall.

2. Position Mylar sheet over the traced design, allowing at least 1" (2.5 cm) border at top and bottom; secure with masking tape. Trace areas that will be stenciled in the first color, using a marking pen; transfer placement lines.

3. Trace design areas for each additional color on a separate Mylar sheet. To help align the design, outline the areas for previous colors, using dotted lines.

4. Layer the Mylar sheets, and check for accuracy. Using mat knife and straightedge, cut outer edges of stencil plates, leaving 1" to 3" (2.5 to 7.5 cm) border around design.

5. Separate sheets. Cut out marked areas on each sheet, using a mat knife; cut the smallest shapes first, then larger ones. Pull knife toward you as you cut, turning the Mylar sheet, rather than the knife, to change the direction.

How to stencil on hard surfaces

1. Mark placement for the stencil on the surface with masking tape. Position the first stencil plate, aligning placement line to tape. Secure the stencil, using masking tape or spray adhesive.

2A. LIQUID PAINT. Place 1 to 2 tsp. (5 to 10 mL) of acrylic or oil-based paint on plastic plate. Dip tip of stencil brush into paint. Using circular motion, blot brush onto folded paper towel until bristles are almost dry.

2B. CRAYON PAINT. Remove protective coating from crayon tip, using paper towel. Rub 1½" (3.8 cm) circle of paint on blank area of stencil plate. Load brush by lightly rubbing brush in circular motion over paint, first in one direction, then in the other.

Continued

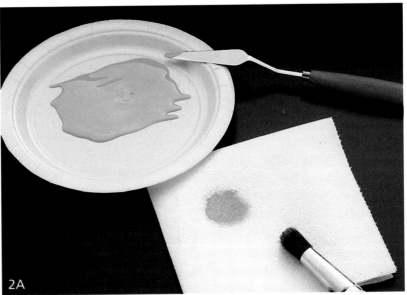

How to stencil on hard surfaces
(CONTINUED)

3A. CIRCULAR METHOD. Hold the brush perpendicular to the surface, and apply paint, using circular motion, within cut areas of stencil. This gives a blended coverage of paint on hard surfaces, such as walls and wood.

3B. STIPPLING METHOD. Apply masking tape around bristles, ¼" (6 mm) from the end. Hold the brush perpendicular to surface, and apply paint using up-and-down motion. This gives a textured appearance on hard surfaces; it is also the technique to use for fabrics.

4. Stencil all cut areas of first stencil plate; allow to dry. Remove plate. Secure second plate to surface, matching the design. Apply second color in all cut areas. Repeat for any remaining stencil plates until design is completed.

5. Touch up any glitches or smudges on surface, using background paint and an artist's brush.

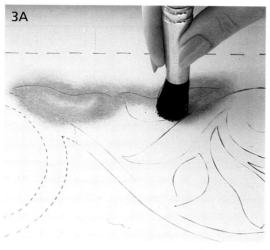

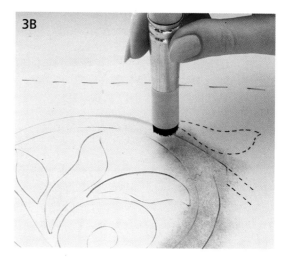

How to stencil on fabrics

1. Prewash fabric to remove any sizing; press fabric. Place fabric, right side up, on medium-grit sandpaper, to keep fabric from shifting. Wrap tape around bristles of stencil brush, ¼" (6 mm) from end.

2. Use undiluted fabric paints or mix two parts craft acrylic paint with one part textile medium. Apply paint to the fabric, using stencil brush and stippling method, as on pages 21 and 22, steps 1 to 5.

3. Heat-set paint when it is thoroughly dry, following the manufacturer's directions for the fabric paint or textile medium that was used; some paints are heat-set from the wrong side of the fabric.

Techniques for shaded designs

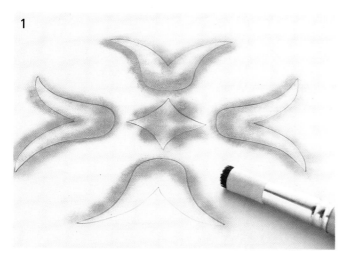

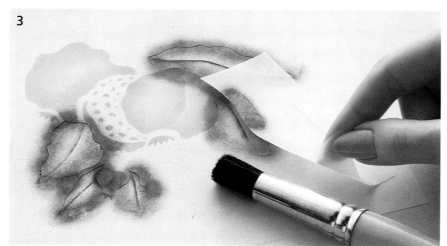

1. Apply paint within cut areas, leaving centers lighter. For an aged, fade-away effect, use a heavier touch at the base of motif and a lighter touch at the top.

2. Apply paint, shading the outer edges of the cut areas, using a complementary or darker color.

3. Apply paint to the outer edges within cut areas; allow to dry. Hold a cut piece of Mylar® in place to cover a portion of the area, and apply paint next to edge of the Mylar; for example, cover one half of a leaf, to stencil the veins.

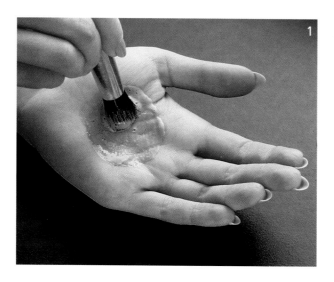

How to clean stencil brushes

1. Apply small amount of dishwashing detergent to stencil brush immediately after stenciling with acrylic paint. Rub the bristles in the palm of your hand in a circular motion, until all paint is removed. Rinse; allow to dry. If oil-based paint is used, clean brushes first, using mineral spirits. Dry on paper towels. Wash with detergent; rinse and allow to dry.

Techniques for turning corners

1. MITERED CORNER. Mask off a diagonal line at corner, using masking tape. Stencil one side up to tape; allow the paint to dry. Reposition the tape over edge of stenciled design. Turn stencil plate, and complete motif.

2. MODIFIED CORNER. Reposition the stencil plate at corners, altering the design as needed around corner. This technique can be used for many curved or loosely connected designs.

3. INTERRUPTED CORNER. Stencil a single pattern in the corner, using a motif slightly larger in width than border design. Stencil the corners first, then fill in the sides.

*S*tenciling Sisal Rugs

Sisal rugs are inexpensive and durable floor coverings with a classic look. As an alternative to either wool or synthetic area rugs, sisal rugs can work well with any decorating style. For a creative touch, sisal rugs can be customized with stenciled designs.

The term *sisal* includes true sisal as well as similar plant fibers, such as coir, jute, rice, sea grass, and maize. True sisal, coir, and jute are coarse fibers and can be rough in texture. The fibers used to make rice, sea grass, and maize rugs are smoother in texture and less abrasive to bare feet. All of the plant fibers can be woven into various patterns, including squares, diamonds, herringbones, and chevrons.

For stenciled designs, select a rug made from coarse fibers, because the paint adheres better to a porous surface. Use acrylic or latex paints, applying the paint with a stencil brush. Designs that are medium-to-large in scale work best due to the rough texture of the rug. Mask off areas to be left unpainted, or use a stencil to paint design motifs.

Before painting a sisal rug or placing furniture on it, unroll the floor covering and let the fibers relax at least 24 hours. Sisal can be placed directly on bare wood, vinyl flooring, or concrete, but you may want to place a nonslip pad under the rug for safety.

INSET PHOTO, OPPOSITE. Sisal is a family of plant fibers that includes: (top row, left to right) true sisal, maize, and sea grass; (bottom row, left to right) rice, jute, and coir. All of these plant fibers can be woven into a variety of patterns.

How to paint borders or stripes on a sisal rug

MATERIALS

- ◆ Rug of porous plant fibers, such as true sisal, coir, or jute.
- ◆ Painter's masking tape.
- ◆ Stencil brush.
- ◆ Acrylic or latex paints.
- ◆ Aerosol clear acrylic sealer.

1. Mask off borders and stripes with painter's masking tape, pressing it firmly to the rug; follow woven rows in the rug whenever possible.

2. Apply paint, using a stencil brush in an up-and-down motion and working the paint into the fibers of the rug. Allow to dry.

3. Remove painter's masking tape. Apply aerosol clear acrylic sealer to the painted area of rug.

How to paint a stenciled design on a sisal rug

MATERIALS

- ◆ Rug of porous plant fibers, such as true sisal, coir, or jute.
- ◆ Painter's masking tape.
- ◆ Stencil plates; stencil brush.
- ◆ Acrylic or latex paints.
- ◆ Aerosol clear acrylic sealer.

1. Plan placement for the design on the entire rug before painting. It may be helpful to position photocopies of stencil plate on the rug to visualize the design and plan the spacing.

2. Tape stencil plate to the rug. Apply paint, using a stencil brush in an up-and-down motion and working the paint into the fibers of the rug.

3. Repeat step 2, using any additional stencil plates. Allow to dry. Apply aerosol clear acrylic sealer to painted area of rug.

Resist-stain Stenciling

Resist-stain stenciling is a technique that can be used on a piece of unfinished furniture to simulate inlaid wood. Stencil the design on the unfinished wood using aerosol clear acrylic sealer. When wood stain is applied to the furniture, the sealed stencil area will not accept the stain, producing a contrasting design in the natural wood tone.

Keep in mind that the wood grain will affect the finished appearance, because any variations in the wood will still be apparent after the stain is applied. For a distinct stencil design, use a clear wood with minimal grain markings.

If desired, the entire piece of furniture can be stained in a light shade before stenciling it, and stained a darker color after the clear acrylic finish is applied to the stenciled area. The stencil design is then the color of the first stain. This technique may be used to create several colors in the stencil, provided each succeeding stain color is darker than the previous one. Pretest the stains and stencil on a scrap of the same type of wood or on the underside of the furniture, to ensure good results.

When applying the aerosol clear acrylic sealer, use several light coats, rather than a few heavy coats , to prevent runs and to keep it from seeping under the stencil plate. Also, whenever possible, place the piece to be stenciled in a horizontal position.

MATERIALS

- Spray adhesive.
- Precut stencil.
- Newspaper; masking tape.
- Aerosol clear acrylic sealer.
- Wood stain.
- Clear acrylic finish, optional.

How to apply a resist-stain stenciled design

1. Apply spray adhesive to the back of pre-cut stencil; allow to dry. Position stencil in the desired location on the unfinished furniture. Press firmly to ensure a tight bond, and cover the surrounding area, using newspaper and masking tape.

2. Apply five or six light coats of aerosol clear acrylic sealer to open areas of the stencil, allowing it to dry thoroughly between coats.

3. Remove the stencil plate. Remove traces of spray adhesive, if any, using lighter fluid. Stain the entire furniture piece; allow it to dry.

4. Apply aerosol clear acrylic sealer or clear finish to the entire furniture piece.

Composite Metallic Stenciling

Wax-based metallic paints can be used to create intriguing stenciled designs. In a technique called composite stenciling, simple individual stencils for each element in the design are repositioned repeatedly as the design is built up. For example, to stencil a bunch of grapes, the design may be built using two or three different circle stencils, varying in size, and two different leaves. Strategic placement and shading of the elements gives the design a three-dimensional appearance. Elements in the foreground are stenciled first, setting up the design lines. Background elements are partially stenciled and shaded to look as if they are behind the foreground elements.

Designs may be stenciled in a single metallic color or in multiple colors, since the wax-based metallic paints are available in a wide variety of colors. A dark base-coat color provides the necessary contrast to the metallic paints for a dramatic effect. Select single stencils, such as leaves, flower petals, fruit, or berries. If desired, cut simple custom stencils (page 20), drawing inspiration from fabric or wallpaper.

How to stencil a composite metallic design

MATERIALS

- Low-luster latex enamel paint or craft acrylic paint in dark color for base coat; sponge applicator or paintbrush.
- Precut or custom stencils.
- Wax-based metallic paints.
- Stencil brush.
- Paper towels.
- Mineral spirits.

1. Prepare surface (page 12). Apply dark base coat; allow to dry. Position first stencil for element in central foreground of design.

2. Pick up small amount of wax-based metallic paint on stencil brush. Distribute paint to bristle ends and remove excess by lightly rubbing brush in circular motion on paper towel, first in one direction, then in the other.

3. Hold the stencil firmly in place with one hand. Hold brush perpendicular to surface and, using circular motion, apply light layer of paint to open area; work around outer edges of stencil first.

4. Continue circular motion of brush, working toward center of stencil with gradually lighter pressure; allow color to fade away near center, creating shaded effect.

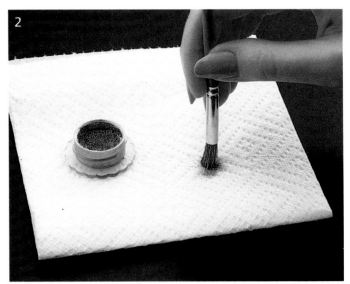

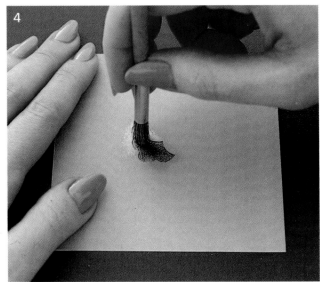

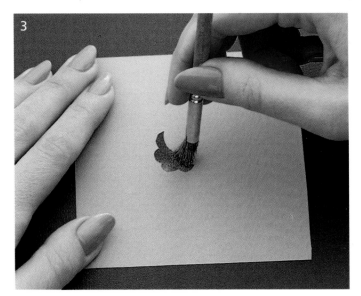

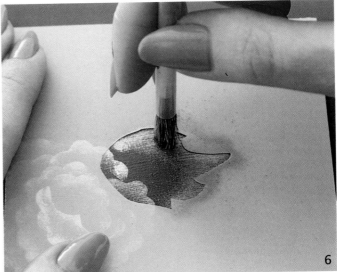

5. Reposition first stencil or position new stencil, and repeat steps 2 to 4; repeat for all elements in foreground of design.

6. Position stencil for element that appears in background, overlapping foreground element. Apply paint as in steps 2 to 4, fading away where the element disappears behind foreground element.

7. Repeat step 6 for all remaining elements of design, stenciling them in the order that they appear, from foreground to the background. Allow to dry. Apply several thin coats of aerosol high-gloss clear acrylic sealer, allowing surface to dry between coats.

8. Clean the stencils by rubbing gently with paper towel dipped in mineral spirits. Clean brush by dipping in mineral spirits and lightly rubbing the brush in a circular motion on paper towel, first in one direction, then in the other.

More ideas for stenciling

OPPOSITE: ARCHITECTURAL DETAILS are enhanced with the use of stenciled borders.

RIGHT: STENCIL, applied beneath cove molding, creates a border.

BOTTOM LEFT: ART DECO MOTIFS embellish a window frame. The interrupted corner treatment adds interest.

BOTTOM RIGHT: RANDOM MOTIFS, adapted from upholstery fabric, decorate an area around a window.

Continued

OPPOSITE COLUMN AND BASEBOARDS are stenciled with coordinating designs for a unified effect.

TOP: BORDER OF VINES AND BERRIES frames the fireplace. The country basket adds a central focal point.

RIGHT: GREEK MOTIFS, surrounded by wall frame molding, add a dramatic accent to a transitional room.

Continued

More ideas for stenciling
(CONTINUED)

OPPOSITE: COUNTRY-STYLE HUTCH is embellished with a stenciled design.

RIGHT: COUNTRY CHAIR features coordinating stencil designs on the wooden chair back and fabric seat cushion.

BOTTOM LEFT: RESIST-STAIN STEN-CILING on this cabinet creates a contrast-ing design.

BOTTOM RIGHT: STENCILED ROD-POCKET CAFES are used for this window treatment.

Continued

OPPOSITE: TRAY is stenciled with a southwestern motif of red peppers.

TOP LEFT: LEAF PINWHEEL DESIGN is applied to the top of a decorative box, using the composite metallic stenciling technique.

TOP RIGHT: FIREPLACE SCREEN features an elaborate stencil of chestnut leaves.

RIGHT: MULTICOLORED COMPOSITE METALLIC STENCILING enhances a picture frame.

BLOCK & SCREEN PRINTING

Block-printed Designs

Block printing is a simple stamping technique that can be used to apply repeated motifs to walls. In this technique, paint is applied to a printing block of wood and foam, then stamped onto the surface to be painted. The block prints can be aligned to form a border, arranged in a set pattern, or scattered randomly.

Closed-cell foam, available at art supply stores and hardware stores, works especially well for making printing blocks, because it cuts easily. Applied to a wood block for easier handling, the closed-cell foam has the necessary flexibility to make clean prints, even on somewhat irregular wall surfaces.

Closed-cell foam is manufactured in several forms. Thin foam sheets with pressure-sensitive backing can be purchased at art supply stores. These are easily cut with scissors into the desired shapes. Another closed-cell foam is neoprene, a synthetic rubber manufactured for use as an insulator. It is commonly available for use as weather stripping in a pressure-sensitive tape, 3/8" (1 cm) thick; however, in this form, the widest tape available is 3/4" (2 cm). Neoprene can also be purchased in sheet form, through suppliers listed in the Yellow Pages under Foam. A computer mouse pad made of neoprene can also be used, although the surface may be textured.

Use acrylic craft paints for block printing on walls. Make a stamp pad for transferring the paint to the printing block by soaking a piece of felt with the paint. A small amount of paint extender increases the open time of the paint, keeping the stamp pad moist longer. It is a good idea to practice with the printing block on paper before printing on the wall, to become familiar with the placement of the design in relation to the outer edge of the block.

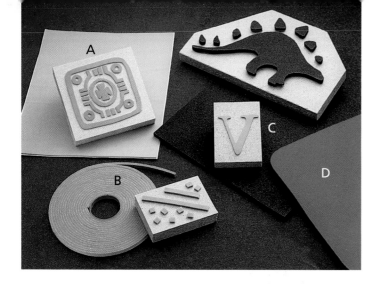

How to make the printing block

Printing blocks are made from closed-cell foam cut to the desired shapes and attached to a wood block. Closed-cell foam is available as A. THIN, PRESSURE-SENSITIVE SHEETS, B. NEOPRENE WEATHER-STRIPPING TAPE, C. NEOPRENE SHEETS, and D. COMPUTER MOUSE PADS.

MATERIALS

- Closed-cell foam, available as thin, pressure-sensitive sheets, pressure-sensitive tape, neoprene sheets, and computer mouse pads.
- Wood block, cut slightly larger than design.
- Acrylic craft paints; acrylic paint extender.
- Felt; sheet of glass or acrylic.
- Craft glue, if foam is not pressure-sensitive.

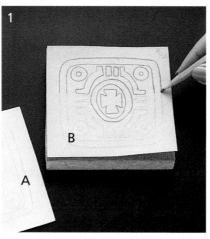

1. Cut tracing paper to same size as the wood block; make pattern for design on tracing paper. Mark top of design on pattern and on edge of block. Transfer design onto the back of the closed-cell foam (A), using graphite paper. Transfer the mirror image of design on underside of wood block (B).

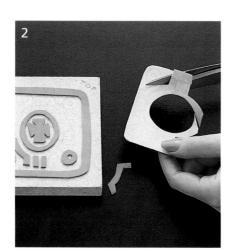

2. Cut the foam on design lines, using scissors. Peel paper from pressure-sensitive backing; affix to the wood block, following the transferred design lines. If using foam without pressure-sensitive backing, affix foam to wood block with craft glue.

3. Glue the original pattern on opposite side of the block, taking care to position it in the same direction as the design on the underside.

How to block-print the design on a wall

1. Mark placement for design motifs on wall, using masking tape or light pencil line. Thin the paint slightly with an acrylic paint extender, about three to four parts paint to one part extender. Cut a piece of felt, larger than printing block; place felt pad on glass or acrylic sheet. Pour the paint mixture onto felt, allowing paint to saturate pad.

2. Press printing block into felt pad, coating surface of foam evenly with paint.

3. Press the printing block to the wall at placement mark, applying firm, even pressure to back of block. Remove the block by pulling it straight back from the wall.

4. Repeat steps 2 and 3 for each block print. Add paint to the felt pad as needed. Touch up any poor impressions, if desired, using a small brush, sponge, or piece of foam.

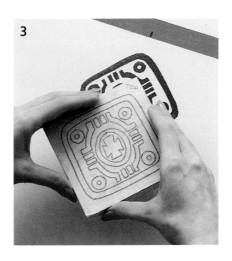

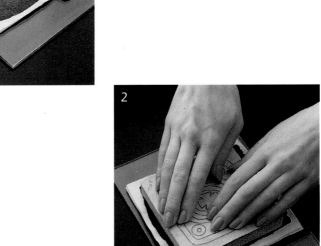

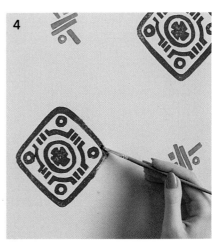

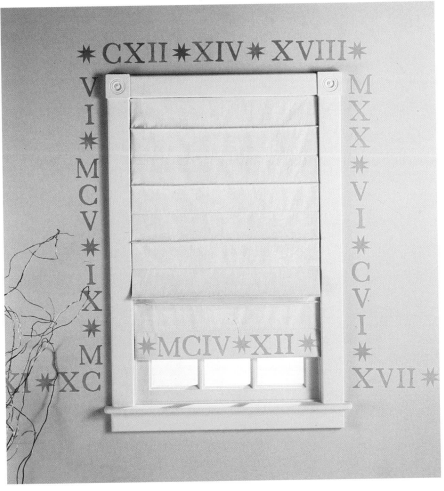

More ideas for block printing

OPPOSITE: DINOSAURS are block-printed randomly across the walls of a child's bedroom.

TOP: TWO-COLOR BORDER is created using a separate block for each color and section of the design.

LEFT: BLOCK-PRINTED BORDER on this stitched-tuck Roman shade matches the border on the wall. To block-print on the fabric, mix two parts of acrylic paint with one part of textile medium, rather than use an extender.

Screen-printed Designs

Screen printing allows you to apply a variety of designs to fabric. In screen printing, ink is forced through a fine screen onto the fabric. The sharp, clear screen-printed designs are quick to produce. It is important to practice screen printing on test fabric to become familiar with the technique and materials.

A special type of screen is used for screen printing. Screens are easy to construct from stretcher bars and polyester mesh. A stencil, cut from Con-Tact® self-adhesive vinyl, is then placed on the screen; when the ink is applied to the screen, it passes through the open cutouts in the stencil.

Use water-based textile inks that are transparent or opaque. The ink may be heat-set, following the manufacturer's directions, for permanent designs that will withstand laundering and dry cleaning.

How to construct a screen for screen printing

MATERIALS

FOR CONSTRUCTING THE SCREEN

- ◆ Four stretcher bars, at least 5″ (12.5 cm) longer than design.
- ◆ 14xx multifilament polyester mesh for most textile inks; 10xx multifilament polyester mesh for white and metallic inks.
- ◆ Masking tape; duct tape, 2″ (5 cm) wide; heavy-duty stapler and ¼″ (6 mm) staples.

1. Assemble the frame from stretcher bars, making sure the corners fit tightly and are squared. Cut mesh 1″ (2.5 cm) larger than the frame on all four sides. Center the mesh over frame, aligning grainlines with sides of the frame.

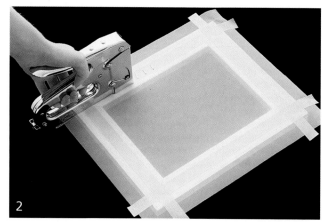

2. Apply masking tape to mesh, about ½″ (1.3 cm) from outer edges of frame. Smooth tape, pressing from center of frame to ends. Staple mesh to frame on one side through masking tape, working from center to ends; place the staples perpendicular to edge of frame, or at a slight diagonal.

3. Staple mesh to opposite side of frame, pulling mesh tight. Repeat for other two sides. Staple corners.

4. Trim excess mesh. Apply duct tape over the masking tape and staples, wrapping tape around sides of frame. Apply duct tape to upper side of screen to form a border, or trough, applying about ½″ (1.3 cm) of tape to the mesh and remainder of the tape to the frame. Stencil design must fit within the taped area.

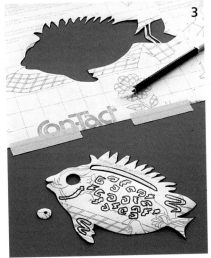

How to prepare the design for screen printing

MATERIALS

FOR PRINTING THE FABRIC

- Fabric, prewashed and pressed.
- Water-based textile inks that are opaque or transparent.
- Con-Tact® self-adhesive vinyl.
- Mat knife; cutting mat; squeegee, 1/2" (1.3 cm) narrower than inside measurement of frame.
- Plastic drop cloth; terry towel; newsprint.

1. Draw or photocopy desired design; design may be enlarged or reduced, using photocopy machine.

2. Hold design up to light source, such as light table or window, and trace design onto paper backing of self-adhesive vinyl.

3. Cut self-adhesive vinyl on design lines, using mat knife.

4. Remove paper backing carefully. Apply vinyl to underside of screen, overlapping duct tape border. Apply cutout details, if any.

5. Turn screen over and press down firmly on the mesh; take care to secure cut edges of the stencil.

How to screen-print the fabric

1. Place plastic drop cloth over the work area, including table and floor. Hang a clothesline to dry prints, if desired. Place terry towel on table over drop cloth; the padded surface helps to produce a better print. Place sheet of newsprint over towel. Place fabric, right side up, over newsprint. Position screen over the fabric.

2. Place 2 to 3 tablespoons (30 to 45 mL) of ink along vinyl next to design area or along border. Applying firm, even pressure, use squeegee to pull ink back and forth across screen until ink is evenly distributed. Too many repetitions cause ink to soak through fabric; too few cause design to look uneven and incomplete.

3. Lift screen slowly to a low angle, taking care that ink does not run onto fabric; carefully peel off fabric. Between prints, rest the screen so one edge is slightly elevated, and rest the squeegee on a stand or lid. Set the screen-printed fabric aside to dry, or hang on a clothesline.

4. Wipe top of the screen gently, using dry facial tissue, if the screen becomes clogged.

5. For final cleanup, remove stencil from screen; wash screen as soon as printing is finished, using soft cloth. Wash off stencil and affix to waxed paper for reuse, if desired.

Toubleshooting problems

1. PRINT IS UNEVEN or incomplete. Too much time may have been taken between prints, or ink may be too thick, causing clogged screen. Thin ink, if necessary, following manufacturer's directions. Wipe clogged screen, opposite.

2. INK RUNS INTO FABRIC along edges of design. Ink was thinned too much, or stencil was not pressed firmly to the screen at edges of design.

3. PRINT HAS UNEVEN PATCHES of color. Ink was applied unevenly, or squeegee was not pulled across screen enough times.

4. INK SOAKS INTO FABRIC. Too much ink was used, or the squeegee was pulled across screen too many times.

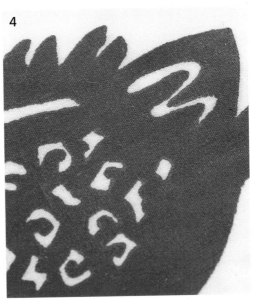

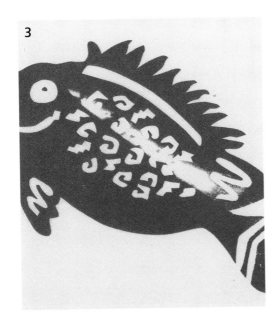

How to make a screen-printed floor cloth

1. Mark canvas to desired size, using pencil, carpenter's square, and straightedge; mark lines in from selvages. Cut canvas. Press canvas so it lies flat. Construct the screen, prepare the design, and screen-print the fabric as on pages 53 to 57.

2. Apply clear acrylic finish, using synthetic-bristle paintbrush; allow to dry several hours. Trim any loose threads at the edges of the floor cloth. Apply two additional coats of clear acrylic finish, applying finish to the edges of canvas, to seal threads.

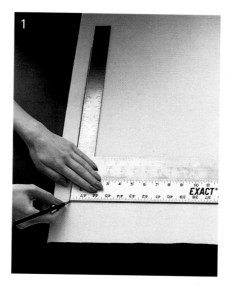

*S*creen-printed *Floor Cloths*

A floor cloth with a custom screen-printed design makes a dramatic decorating statement at a low cost. For the screen printing, you may want to duplicate a design used elsewhere in the room, such as a fabric or wallcovering design, or use any design with a simple shape that can be cut out easily to make the screen.

An 18-oz. (500 g) or #8 canvas provides a durable surface for floor cloths and lies flat on the floor. It is available in widths up to 5 ft. (152.5 cm) at tent and awning stores and upholstery shops. After it is screen-printed, protect the floor cloth by sealing it with a clear acrylic finish. The sealed floor cloth may be cleaned by wiping it with a wet towel. If the floor cloth is used on a smooth floor surface, such as a wood floor, place a nonslip pad underneath it.

MATERIALS

- Materials for constructing the screen, as on page 54.
- Materials for printing the fabric, as on page 55.
- 18-oz. (500 g) or #8 canvas.
- Clear acrylic finish: synthetic-bristle paintbrush.

More ideas for screen printing

OPPOSITE: FUTON MATTRESS is slip-covered with screen-printed fabric for a truly unique look.

TOP: BOLD STRIPES in primary colors are screen printed on a cheerful floor cloth.

RIGHT: SCREEN-PRINTED SEASHELLS adorn the lower edge of a fabric roller shade.

Index

CY DECOSSE INCORPORATED

President/COO: Nino Tarantino
Executive V.P./Editor-in-Chief: William B. Jones
Chairman Emeritus: Cy DeCosse

Creative Touches™
Group Executive Editor: Zoe A. Graul
Managing Editor: Elaine Johnson
Editor: Linda Neubauer
Associate Creative Director: Lisa Rosenthal
Senior Art Director: Delores Swanson
Contributing Art Director: Judith Meyers
Computer Design: Mark Jacobson
Copy Editor: Janice Cauley
Desktop Publishing Specialist: Laurie Kristensen
Sample Production Manager: Carol Olson
Studio Manager: Marcia Chambers
Print Production Manager: Patt Sizer

COWLES
Enthusiast Media

President/COO: Philip L. Penny

STENCILING ETC.
Created by: The Editors of Cy DeCosse Incorporated

Also available in the Creative Touches™ series:

*Sponging Etc., Stone Finishes Etc., Valances Etc.,
Painted Designs Etc., Metallic Finishes Etc., Swags Etc.,
Papering Projects Etc.*

The Creative Touches™ series draws from the individual titles of
The Home Decorating Institute®. Individual titles are also available
from the publisher and in bookstores and fabric stores.

Printed on American paper by:
  R. R. Donnelley & Sons Co.
99 98 97 96 / 5 4 3 2 1

Cy DeCosse Incorporated offers a variety of how-to books.

For information write:
  Cy DeCosse Subscriber Books
  5900 Green Oak Drive
  Minnetonka, MN 55343